"Discovering Your Potential: Embracing Life's Boundless Opportunities"

Grover ASEQUIA

BookLeaf
Publishing

India | USA | UK

Presentation by *BookLeaf Publishing*

Web: www.bookleafpub.com

E-mail: info@bookleafpub.com

ISBN: 9789358734683

First edition 2023

DEDICATION

To all the dreamers, seekers, and believers who refuse to settle for mediocrity and instead choose to embrace the full spectrum of life's boundless opportunities. May you unleash your potential, pursue your passions, and create a life that embodies your deepest desires. This book "Discovering Your Potential: Embracing Life's Boundless Opportunities" is dedicated to my family, especially to my wife Gemmafe Asequia, Blue Gevermmy, Grayver Kenan, my kids and to my readers, with admiration and unwavering faith in your ability to create your own extraordinary journey.

To God be all the glory.

Grover

ACKNOWLEDGEMENT

I would like to express my heartfelt gratitude to all those who have contributed to the creation of "Discovering Your Potential: Embracing Life's Boundless Opportunities", especially to my wife, Gemmafe, kids, Grayver Kenan and Blue Gevermmy and Mary Claire. Your unwavering support, encouragement, and belief in this project have been instrumental in its realization. Thank you for joining me on this journey of personal growth and empowerment and for inspiring others to embrace the limitless possibilities that life offers.

With sincere appreciation,

Grover

PREFACE

Within the pages of this compilation, you will find a collection of poems that have emerged from the depths of my heart and soul. Each verse is a reflection of my emotions, experiences, and observations, woven together in an intricate tapestry of words. This compilation is a testament to the power of poetry, which has the ability to capture the essence of our human existence and evoke profound emotions.

As a poet, my intention is to create a space where readers can delve into the realms of imagination, introspection, and empathy. These poems explore themes of Embracing Life's Boundless Opportunities. Through lyrical language and vivid imagery, I hope to transport you to a place of reflection and connection with the universal human experience.

It is my deepest desire that these poems resonate with you, that they awaken something within you—a spark of recognition, a moment of solace, or a newfound perspective. May this compilation serve as an invitation to embrace the beauty of poetry, to explore the depths of your own emotions, and to find solace and inspiration in the written word.

With heartfelt gratitude,

Grover Asequia

On Time and Memory

I've kept with me stanzas, for my fairest and
dearest Sampaguita.
Whose beauty is so unparalleled that sailors and
travelers
Conquer mountains and waves for a mere glance
of her beauty.

But even the most fragrant flowers reek when
sniffed with greed.

These voyagers were never her saviors. They
filled her with promises and lies.
In the end she grappled alone to save her life.

Such was the fate of Sampaguita, who begged
for time to bury it all behind.
But alas, she has to pay the cost of time.

What a pity and a cruel thing
For Sampaguita to be so forgetful and forgiving
To once again bloom for greed and cruelty
And allow time to bury what you fought for in
forgotten memory

Oh Sampaguita, how I ache for you

You've turned a blind eye to this regime, a creeping history
Will it be too late to realize
That this time, the voyagers are no longer the enemy.

Silent Suffering

In this forest that I have grown,
Where secrets lie and shadows are sown,
I've cared for and cultivated each tree,
Yet the mystery of its suffering eludes me.

No fire scorched these leafy boughs,
But time slipped away, silently it prowls,
Like a lurking plague, unseen, unknown,
Leaving scars deep within, where pain has
grown.

Did they call out to me, a voice so faint?
Or was I too deaf, my senses feigned?
Lost in my own world, I failed to perceive,
The silent pleas of a forest that grieved.

Now, as I wander within its embrace,
I sense the anguish, the sorrow I face,
For far too long, it silently endured,
Its suffering veiled, its agony obscured.

Each tree whispers its story to me,
The ache it carried, longing to be free,
I listen now, attuned to its plight,
Seeking redemption in the forest's night.

With eyes wide open, I delve into the past,
Unraveling the enigmas that were cast,
Through layers of time, I begin to see,
The truth that was obscured, waiting to be set free.

No longer blind to the forest's pain,
I witness its scars, the tears like rain,
In this journey of shadows and light,
I find solace and purpose, reclaiming what's right.

Together, we heal, the forest and I,
With love and compassion, we'll pacify,
The wounds that lingered for far too long,
Restoring harmony with a hopeful song.

In this forest I have grown, I'll sow anew,
Nurturing its beauty, its spirit true,
No longer blind, I'll tend with care,
Guided by love, this forest we'll repair.

Open Your Eyes to Infinite Possibilities

Open your eyes and let your vision soar
There's so much to discover, so much more.
Open your eyes, embrace the unknown
The possibilities are yours to own.

Open your eyes to endless dreams
Where imagination dances and gleams.
Open your eyes to the beauty around
In every sight, a treasure can be found.

Open your eyes to different perspectives
Learn from others, connect and be receptive.
Open your eyes to empathy and grace
Understanding others, their unique space.

Open your eyes to growth and change
Embrace challenges, they're not so strange.
Open your eyes to new beginnings
Transforming obstacles into meaningful
winnings.

Open your eyes to love and compassion
Spread kindness, create a ripple of passion.
Open your eyes to the power you possess

To make a difference, to leave an imprint, no
less.

Open your eyes to the vastness of your soul
Unleash your potential, make yourself whole.
Open your eyes, my dear friend, and see
The world is waiting, full of possibility.

Every Time I Look at You

In your eyes, I find peace,
A sense of belonging that will never cease.
With every glance, my worries subside,
And in your presence, I can confide.

You bring a light to my darkest days,
A warmth that sets my heart ablaze.
Through life's challenges, you're my guiding star,
Always there to remind me who you are.

Your unwavering support and care,
Wrap me in a love beyond compare.
In your embrace, I find strength and trust,
A refuge where my fears are hushed.

Though doubts may cloud my mind at times,
Your love shines through like vibrant chimes.
Together, we navigate the unknown,
Building a bond that has only grown.

Every time I look at you, my dear,
I'm reminded that love is always near.
Through highs and lows, our connection is true,
And I'm forever grateful for you.

The Reality of Me

To those who mock and jest,
I stand tall, unaffected by your test.

To those who love and embrace,
Your acceptance fuels my inner grace.

To those who lend a helping hand,
Your kindness, I truly understand.

To those I've hurt along the way,
I humbly ask for forgiveness today.

To those I've supported and uplifted,
May understanding be reciprocated, unscripted.

To those I've failed to assist,
With empathy, let our bond persist.

To those who brighten my every day,
You've painted my world in a vibrant display.

In the Realm of Self

To those who scoff and jeer,
I stand firm, your words won't adhere.

To those who cherish and hold dear,
Your love embraces me, crystal clear.

To those who lend their helping hand,
Your support, a beacon on life's sand.

To those I've wronged with thoughtless ways,
I humbly seek your forgiveness, through the
haze.

To those I've aided with compassion's might,
I hope you find solace in my guiding light.

To those I've overlooked, neglected in need,
May understanding bridge the gap, indeed.

To those whose presence completes my day,
Gratitude flows, like a sun's warm ray.

The Love of My Life

In a world where love dances, free and true,
There blooms a story, I must share with you.
Through the winds of time, our paths aligned,
A love so rare, forever intertwined.

In your eyes, I find the stars' gentle gleam,
A universe of passion, it would seem.
Your smile, a beacon, guiding my way,
Brightening each moment, come what may.

Your touch, a gentle caress on my soul,
Ignites a fire, making me feel whole.
With every heartbeat, our love takes flight,
A symphony of emotions, pure and bright.

In your embrace, I find solace and peace,
A sanctuary where all worries cease.
Together we journey, hand in hand,
Through life's challenges, we bravely stand.

You're the melody that sings in my heart,
The missing piece, the masterpiece of art.
In your love, I've discovered pure bliss,
My forever love, my eternal kiss.

In the Eyes of a Child

In the eyes of a child, wonders unfold,
A world of innocence, pure and untold.
With curiosity as their guiding light,
They embark on adventures, day and night.

Their laughter echoes through the air,
Like melodies of joy, beyond compare.
Their hearts are filled with boundless love,
A gift bestowed from the heavens above.

In the mind of a child, dreams take flight,
Imagination soars to unimaginable height.
They build castles in the sand and skies,
Unfolding stories with each heartfelt sigh.

Their spirits untouched by cynicism's sting,
They dance with hope, on fragile wings.
In their presence, worries seem to fade,
As they embrace life's every serenade.

Oh, the beauty of a child's embrace,
Their gentle touch, a tender grace.
They teach us to cherish and believe,
In the magic that life can still conceive.

So let us learn from these little souls,
To keep our hearts open, reaching our goals.
For in the eyes of a child, we find,
The purest essence of humankind

The Love of Eternity

In love's eternal embrace we find,
A bond that lasts throughout all time.
No limits, no boundaries, it knows no end,
A love that forever transcends.

Across the universe, it soars and sings,
Touching hearts with the joy it brings.
In every moment, it holds us near,
A love that's constant, crystal clear.

It fills our days with warmth and light,
Guiding us through both day and night.
Through highs and lows, it remains steadfast,
A love that forever shall last.

So let us cherish this love so true,
A gift that's meant for me and you.
In the love of eternity, we are blessed,
Forever united, eternally caressed.

The Land of Bounty

The United States, land of bounty wide,
Where nature's gifts and riches reside.
From rolling plains to majestic peaks,
A land of plenty that endlessly speaks.

Vast fields stretch far and wide,
Where crops grow tall with fertile pride.
Golden corn and wheat fields sway,
Feeding the nation day by day.

Rivers flow with waters pure,
Teeming with life, a vibrant lure.
Fish and wildlife, a bountiful sight,
Nature's treasures, a pure delight.

From sea to shining sea, a diverse land,
With landscapes varied and grand.
Mountains high and valleys low,
The beauty of nature, for all to know.

And in the cities, a bustling scene,
Opportunities abundant, dreams to glean.
Innovation and progress, a constant drive,
A beacon of hope, where dreams thrive.

But amidst the bounty, let's not forget,
The importance of sharing, without regret.
To care for the land and all that it gives,
Ensuring its bounty forever lives.

The United States, a land of plenty,
Where abundance and opportunity aplenty.
Let's treasure this land, with gratitude and care,
For the bounty it offers, beyond compare.

The Horizon Far from Home

On the horizon, far from home,
A world unknown, yet beckoning to roam.
Beyond familiar sights and familiar skies,
Adventure awaits, where the heart flies.

The sun sets, painting hues of gold,
Casting shadows of stories yet untold.
In the distance, dreams come alive,
Beyond the known, where new paths thrive.

Leaving behind the comforts we've known,
We step into the vast and the unknown.
With every step, a new chapter unfolds,
Where destinies are shaped and stories are told.

The horizon calls with whispers and sighs,
Promising wonders beneath boundless skies.
New cultures, new faces, and unfamiliar lands,
Weaving memories with delicate hands.

Though the road may be long and the journey
unknown,
The horizon's allure continues to be shown.
For it holds the promise of growth and change,
As we venture into the world's wide range.

The Lesson of Life

Life is a tapestry woven with threads,
Lessons and experiences, filling our heads.
Each day we're given a chance to learn,
To grow, to evolve, and to take our turn.

Lessons come in various forms,
Through triumph and failure, calm and storms.
They teach us resilience, patience, and grace,
And challenge us to find our rightful place.

The lesson of life is to embrace change,
To navigate the unknown and rearrange.
For growth lies outside our comfort zone,
Where new opportunities are sown.

We learn the power of love and compassion,
To uplift others and find satisfaction.
To be kind, empathetic, and forgiving,
And create a world that is truly living.

Life teaches us the value of time,
To seize the moments, both sublime and prime.
To cherish connections, both old and new,
And appreciate the beauty in all we pursue.

We learn to find strength in our darkest hour,
To rise above adversity with inner power.
To never lose hope, even in despair,
For life's challenges, we're equipped to bear.

The lesson of life is to follow our dreams,
To pursue passions with unwavering beams.
To listen to our hearts and trust our intuition,
And manifest a life of purposeful fruition.

So let us embrace the lessons that life imparts,
And approach each day with open hearts.
For in the journey of life, we find our way,
Growing wiser, stronger, with each passing day.

Embracing the Value of Time

In the realm of time, a precious gift,
Lies a treasure that causes spirits to lift.
For in its essence, lies a secret profound,
A poet's muse, a philosopher's ground.

Time, the great equalizer, marching on,
Weaves its tapestry, from dusk till dawn.
Moments fleeting, slipping through our hands,
Yet their worth, we fail to understand.

The value of time, a poem shall convey,
Its message clear, like the break of day.
Each ticking second, an opportunity,
To shape our lives, with purpose and unity.

In youth's embrace, we often linger,
Lost in dreams, our aspirations eager.
But time whispers softly, a gentle plea,
"Seize the moments, for they make you free."

As the years unfold, like petals in bloom,
Time's wisdom dances in each crowded room.
For it teaches patience, resilience, and grace,
Guiding us forward, at our own chosen pace.

Yet time is finite, a resource so rare,
No riches or power can ever compare.
No wealth can buy it, nor magic extend,
A life well-lived, time's true dividend.

So let us cherish the moments we're blessed,
Embrace their essence, and give them our best.
For the value of time lies not in its length,
But in the love, we share, and the strength we
extend.

Live with intention, embrace each new day,
For time, like a river, will soon slip away.
So seize the present, in its fleeting prime,
And honor the value of time, sublime.

Regime's Bone

Perhaps it was last summer
When all lights went out in the village.
No one questioned.
Or maybe, no one dared.

After all, one befriends darkness to hide
something ugly
But at night when the world is asleep,
The wind brings forth a faint lullaby…

Hear out the plea
A cry of anger and disbelief
The regime's bones
Our ugly history

Soft and slow, drawing me in
The song of the regime's bones
A lullaby of truth
A blessing to be known
But a curse to sing along

Perhaps it was last summer
When we turned our backs to a junkyard of
bones
The bones that carried our history

Remnants of how we fought for our truths and
liberty

You want to sing along? Is the lullaby haunting?
Are the truths choking you?
Such is the cost of knowledge
Such is the cost of listening
To the cry of the regime's bones.

Will I End Up Like This?

Flash!
Camera flashes to capture the scene,
Freezing a moment in time, forever keen.
Amidst the darkness, a vivid red hue,
Revealing a life extinguished, a tragedy so true.

The clicking sound as I write,
Echoes like a ticking clock, day and night.
Each keystroke feels like a countdown,
A reminder of the secrets I've found.

Fear grips my heart, tight and heavy,
As I confront the truth, silent and deadly.
For it has the power to cost me greatly,
To strip away my name or my liberty.

Or perhaps it's not just my own fate,
But the lives of others hanging in the balance, I
contemplate.
Will this flashing light expose their lies?
Revealing the hidden darkness, causing their
demise?

Flash! The truth flashes before my eyes,
A prism of revelations, a web of lies.

Each glimmer holds a piece of the puzzle,
A truth so fragile, yet impossible to muzzle.

In the depths of uncertainty, I tread,
Seeking solace, grappling with dread.
For this truth, though powerful, comes at a cost,
In a world where the line between justice and
chaos is lost.

The camera flash fades, but the aftermath
remains,
A haunting reminder of life's relentless strains.
In the pursuit of truth, I stand resolute,
Navigating the shadows, walking a path
absolute.

With each revelation, the canvas reveals,
The interconnectedness of wounds that never
heal.
For in this journey, I unveil not only their deceit,
But the strength within me, refusing to retreat.

Flash! The final chapter is yet to be told,
As the truth unravels, fearless and bold.
With pen in hand, I'll document the tale,
Exposing the darkness, allowing justice to
prevail.

In the end, the flashing light becomes a beacon,

Guiding me forward, though the path is
unforeseen.
For within the shadows, where secrets reside,
Lies the power to change, to heal, and to stride.

I Am

Within me reside the fragments of souls,
Those once encountered, those who played their
roles.
From chance meetings to fleeting connections,
A symphony of beings, shaping my reflections.

I am a living map, roads etched on my skin,
Each path traversed, a story held within.
The places I have ventured, imprinted in my
heart,
A tapestry of landscapes, shaping every part.

A photo album of moments lived and shared,
A kaleidoscope of memories, cherished and
cared.
In each snapshot lies a glimpse of my past,
A mosaic of experiences, a legacy that will last.

I am a mirror, reflecting the shades of me,
A reflection of who I was, who I longed to be.
A history book, pages filled with countless
versions,
Each chapter, an evolution, marking my
transformations.

As a whole, I am an intricate design,
Revealing glimpses of moments that define me.
In scattered fragments, I've scattered parts of my soul,
In secret corners, where I found solace, whole.

Within these pieces, I find a sense of grace,
A compilation of fragments, woven into place.
I am the sum of these fragments, uniquely entwined,
An amalgamation of existence, eternally refined.

In the moments I've experienced, the lives I've touched,
In the tapestry of connections, I am flushed.
Every fragment solidified, forming a unified whole,
Each piece a testament to the story that I hold.

I am the culmination of these fragments divine,
An ever-evolving mosaic, a reflection so fine.
A symphony of existence, crafted with care,
All these fragments, my entirety I declare

A Precious Gift From God

In tiny hands and sparkling eyes,
A world of wonder and surprise,
My child, a treasure in my sight,
Filling my days with pure delight.

A smile that brightens up my soul,
A heart that's pure, making me whole,
In every giggle, I find pure bliss,
A tiny being I wouldn't dare to miss.

Your laughter dances like a gentle breeze,
Bringing warmth and joy with ease,
With innocence and curiosity so sweet,
You make my life feel complete.

In your eyes, I see a future bright,
A world of dreams, shining so light,
With every step, you learn and grow,
Unfolding a story we're yet to know.

You fill my days with boundless love,
A blessing sent from high above,
In your embrace, I find endless grace,
A precious gift, my child, you are my embrace

Eternal Love

In her eyes, a universe resides,
A love that forever abides,
My wife, my heart's eternal flame,
A blessing beyond any name.

With a touch, she lights my soul,
Her presence makes me whole,
In her embrace, I find solace and peace,
A love that will never cease.

Her laughter, a melody so sweet,
In her smile, my heart finds its beat,
Through life's journey, hand in hand,
Together, we'll forever stand.

In her strength, I find courage anew,
In her wisdom, a love so true,
She's my rock, my guiding light,
My love for her shines ever bright.

In her love, I've found my home,
A love that's deep, a love that's grown,
Forever grateful for her by my side,
With her, my love will forever reside.

9 789358 734683